Good Housekeeping

Pasta

HEARST BOOKS

A Division of Sterling Publishing Co., Inc.

New York

GOOD HOUSEKEEPING
Ellen Levine   Editor in Chief
Susan Westmoreland   Food Director
Susan Deborah Goldsmith   Associate Food Director
Delia Hammock   Nutrition Director
Sharon Franke   Food Appliances Director
Richard Eisenberg   Special Projects Director
Marilu Lopez   Design Director

Photography Credits
Brian Hagiwara: pages 8, 15, 20, and 28.
Ann Stratton: pages 11 and 16.
Alan Richardson: pages 7, 19, and 24.
Mark Thomas: pages 1, 3, 12, 23, and 27.

Supplemental Text by Anne Wright

Book design by Liz Trovato

The recipes in this book have been excerpted from *Good Housekeeping 100 Best Pasta Recipes*.

2 4 6 8 10 9 7 5 3 1

Published by Hearst Books
A Division of Sterling Publishing Company, Inc.
387 Park Avenue South, New York, NY 10016

Good Housekeeping is a trademark owned by Hearst Magazines Property, Inc., in USA, and Hearst Communications, Inc., in Canada. Hearst Books is a trademark owned by Hearst Communications, Inc.

The Good Housekeeping Cookbook Seal guarantees that the recipes in this Cookbook meet the strict standards of the Good Housekeeping Institute. Every recipe has been triple-tested for ease, reliability, and great taste.

www.goodhousekeeping.com

Distributed in Canada by Sterling Publishing
c/o Canadian Manda Group, 165 Dufferin Street
Toronto, Ontario, Canada M6K 3H6
Distributed in Australia by Capricorn Link (Australia) Pty. Ltd.
P.O. Box 704, Windsor, NSW 2756 Australia

Printed in China

ISBN 1-58816-540-X

Contents

Great Pasta, Every Time

Perfectly cooked pasta is firm yet tender to the bite, or *al dente* as Italians say, with sauce coating each delicious mouthful. Some of the most common mistakes—mushy spaghetti, watery lasagna, sauce that pools in the bottom of the bowl instead of clinging to the noodle—can easily be avoided by following a few simple guidelines.

For best taste and texture, look for pasta, either Italian or American, made from durum wheat flour or semolina flour. Choose pasta packaged in cardboard boxes. The cardboard keeps out light, which can destroy riboflavin, an important nutrient found in pasta. Resist the urge to transfer pasta from the box to a clear decorative container—the original box offers better protection.

Store dried pasta in a cool, dark place for up to a year. Whole-wheat pasta has a shorter shelf life: no longer than six months and sometimes less. Read package instructions to be sure. Fresh pasta should be refrigerated according to package directions, usually for up to a week. It can also be frozen for up to a month. It's best NOT to thaw frozen pasta before cooking.

Use plenty of boiling water. A good rule of thumb is 4 quarts for each pound of pasta. Bring it to a rolling boil (covering the pot hastens the process), then add about 2 teaspoons of salt per pound of pasta. Salted water takes longer to boil, so add the salt just before adding the pasta. Don't be tempted to omit the salt, it's essential for proper seasoning.

Stir frequently to prevent sticking. Once you've salted the water and it's at a full boil, stir in the pasta. Cover the pot, if necessary, to return water quickly to a boil. Uncover and continue cooking, stirring often until the strands separate. There's no need to add oil to pasta cooking water. In fact, the oil might keep the sauce from adhering to the pasta. Stirring is all you need to prevent sticking.

Cook according to package directions. There's no set rule for how long each pasta shape should cook. Spaghetti from one manufacturer may take longer than the same size spaghetti from another, depending on the type of wheat used and how it was processed. So always read the box—it will give you the correct cooking time.

Check for doneness often before the suggested cooking time has elapsed. The goal is pasta that's tender yet still slightly firm or *al dente*. The only way to test it is by tasting. Remove a piece from the pot and rinse it briefly under warm water, then taste. There should be no hard white center. Remember that the pasta will continue cooking from the residual heat even after draining. If the cooked pasta will be baked later, undercook it slightly.

Drain well in a colander, shaking to make sure all excess water has been removed. Don't rinse pasta unless the recipe specifies to do so. Rinsing can remove starch that helps the sauce cling and provides important nutrients.

Pasta: The Long and Short of It

The recipes in this book use a variety of pastas. In most cases, particularly if a shape is not common, the ingredients list will suggest an easily found substitution. If you don't recognize the particular pasta called for in a recipe, this glossary tells you what to look for.

Long strands

Capellini: Sometimes called "angel hair." Very thin spaghetti.
Fusilli: Long, wavy strands, "corkscrew pasta."
Spaghetti: Long, thin round strands.
Vermicelli: Very thin spaghetti.

Flat ribbons

Egg noodles: Short, flat, and slightly curled when dry. No-yolk versions are widely available.
Fettuccine: Flat noodles, 1/4 inch wide.
Lasagna: Wide, flat pasta. Available in "no-cook" form.
Linguine: Thin pasta ribbons, 1/8 inch wide.
Mafalda: Wide ribbons with a ruffled edge.
Tagliatelle: A little wider than fettuccine.

Tubular pastas

Elbow macaroni: Small curved tubular pasta.
Penne: Pasta tubes with diagonal ends.
Rigatoni: Large ribbed tubes.
Ziti: Medium tubes.

Small pastas

Campanelle: Tiny bell-shaped pasta.
Cavatappi: Small corkscrews.
Ditalini: Short tubular pasta; also called tubettini.
Orechini: Pasta "earrings."
Orzo: Rice-shaped pasta.

One-of-a-kind pastas

Cavatelli: Short ridged pasta.
Conchiglie: Medium shells.
Creste di gallo: Curved pasta with ridged edge.
Farfalle: Literal translation is "butterflies"; known in America as bow ties.
Gemelli: Two short strands of pasta that have been twisted together.
Manicotti: Large tubes of pasta for stuffing.
Orecchiette: Small rounded pasta disks; literal translation is "little ears."
Radiatore: Shaped like small radiators.
Rotini: Corkscrew shape. Also called rotelle.
Ruote: Wagon wheel-shaped pasta.
Stelline: Tiny star-shaped pasta.

Stuffed pastas

Picrogi: Round Polish pasta dumplings, filled with meat, potatoes, or cheese.
Ravioli: Plump pasta pillows filled with cheese or with meat.
Tortellini: Small pasta rings filled with cheese or with meat.

Asian noodles

Cellophane noodles: Also called bean threads or *mai fun*.
Chinese-style egg noodles: Wheat-flour noodles that are similar to egg linguine.
Rice sticks: Very thin noodles that are cooked by soaking or deep frying.
Soba: Thin brownish noodles made from buckwheat flour.
Udon noodles: Long, thick, chewy Japanese wheat-flour noodles.

Lentil and Macaroni Soup

PREP 20 MINUTES   COOK 50 MINUTES   MAKES ABOUT 12 CUPS OR 6 SERVINGS

Macaroni makes this dish a surefire hit with young eaters. Pass shredded mozzarella cheese for a kid-friendly topping.

1	tablespoon olive oil
2	medium carrots, cut into 1/4-inch dice
1	medium onion, chopped
2	garlic cloves, crushed with garlic press
1	can (141/2 ounces) whole tomatoes in puree
1	can (141/2 ounces) vegetable broth
3/4	cup dry lentils, rinsed
1/2	teaspoon salt
1/2	teaspoon coarsely ground black pepper
1/4	teaspoon dried thyme
6	cups water
1	bunch Swiss chard (about 1 pound), trimmed and coarsely chopped
3/4	cup elbow macaroni (about 31/2 ounces)
1	cup fresh basil leaves, chopped
	grated Parmesan cheese (optional)

• In nonstick 5- to 6-quart Dutch oven, heat oil over medium heat until hot. Add carrots, onion, and garlic, and cook 10 minutes or until vegetables are tender and golden, stirring occasionally. Add tomatoes with their puree, broth, lentils, salt, pepper, thyme, and water; heat to boiling, stirring to break up tomatoes with side of spoon. Reduce heat to low; cover and simmer 20 minutes or until lentils are almost tender.

• Stir in Swiss chard and macaroni; heat to boiling over medium-high heat. Reduce heat to medium; cook, uncovered, about 10 minutes or until macaroni is tender. Stir in basil. Serve with Parmesan, if you like.

Each serving: About 200 calories, 12 g protein, 34 g carbohydrate, 3 g total fat (0 g saturated), 0 mg cholesterol, 810 mg sodium.

Test Kitchen Tip

Unlike most other legumes, lentils need no presoaking. Just rinse them thoroughly in a colander and pick through them to remove any stones or shriveled lentils.

Pasta Salad with Lemon and Peas

PREP 20 MINUTES   COOK 20 MINUTES   MAKES ABOUT 10 CUPS OR 12 ACCOMPANIMENT SERVINGS

This super simple salad makes a nice change from potato salad at picnics. Try it with anything from chicken to grilled steak.

1	pound bow-tie or small shell pasta
1	package (10 ounces) frozen baby peas
2	lemons
2/3	cup milk
1/2	cup light mayonnaise
1	teaspoon salt
1/4	teaspoon coarsely ground black pepper
1	cup loosely packed fresh basil leaves, chopped
4	green onions, thinly sliced

- In large saucepot, cook pasta as label directs, adding frozen peas during last 2 minutes of cooking time. Drain pasta and peas; rinse with cold water and drain well.

- Meanwhile, from lemons, grate 1 tablespoon peel and squeeze 3 tablespoons juice. In large bowl, with wire whisk, mix lemon peel and juice with milk, mayonnaise, salt, pepper, basil, and green onions until blended.

- Add pasta and peas to mayonnaise dressing; toss to coat well. Cover and refrigerate up to two days if not serving right away.

Each serving: About 207 calories, 7 g protein, 33 g carbohydrate, 4 g total fat (1 g saturated), 5 mg cholesterol, 327 mg sodium.

Radiatore with Arugula, Tomatoes, and Pancetta

PREP 15 MINUTES   COOK 15 MINUTES   MAKES 4 MAIN-DISH OR 8 ACCOMPANIMENT SERVINGS

Here's a BLT Italian-style—pasta replaces the bread, arugula replaces the lettuce, and pancetta replaces the bacon. So easy, so good.

1	package (16 ounces) radiatore or corkscrew pasta
4	ounces sliced pancetta or bacon, cut into 1/4-inch pieces (see Tip)
1	garlic clove, crushed with garlic press
1	container (16 ounces) cherry tomatoes, each cut into quarters
1/2	teaspoon salt
1/4	teaspoon coarsely ground black pepper
8	ounces arugula or spinach, tough stems removed
1/4	cup grated Parmesan cheese
	shredded Parmesan cheese for garnish

- In large saucepot, prepare pasta as label directs.

- Meanwhile, in 10-inch skillet, cook the pancetta over medium heat until lightly browned, stirring occasionally. (If using bacon, discard all but 1 tablespoon fat.) Add garlic; cook 30 seconds, stirring. Add tomatoes, salt, and pepper, and cook 1 to 2 minutes. Remove skillet from heat; cover and keep warm.

- Drain the pasta; return to saucepot. Add pancetta mixture, arugula, and grated Parmesan cheese; toss well. Garnish with shredded Parmesan cheese.

Each main-dish serving: About 560 calories, 22 g protein, 93 g carbohydrate, 12 g total fat (4 g saturated), 15 mg cholesterol, 680 mg sodium.

Test Kitchen Tip

Pancetta, an Italian bacon, is cured in a mixture of salt and spices. Unlike American bacon, it is not smoked so its flavor is somewhat milder. Look for it in Italian markets, specialty meats shops, or large supermarkets. If you can't find it, use bacon.

Seafood Fra Diavolo

A tempting mix of squid, mussels, and shrimp in a robust tomato sauce. Simply add garlic bread and a green salad and dinner is ready.

8	ounces cleaned squid
1	tablespoon olive oil
1	large garlic clove, finely chopped
1/4	teaspoon crushed red pepper
1	can (28 ounces) plum tomatoes
1/2	teaspoon salt
1	dozen mussels, scrubbed and debearded (see Tip)
8	ounces medium shrimp, shelled and deveined
1	package (16 ounces) linguine or spaghetti
1/4	cup chopped fresh parsley

• Rinse squid and pat dry with paper towels. Slice squid bodies crosswise into 1/4-inch rings. Cut tentacles into several pieces if they are large.

• In nonreactive 4-quart saucepan, heat oil over medium heat. Add garlic and crushed red pepper; cook just until fragrant, about 30 seconds. Stir in tomatoes with their juice and salt, breaking up tomatoes with side of spoon. Heat to boiling over high heat. Add squid and heat to boiling. Reduce heat; cover and simmer 30 minutes. Remove cover and simmer 15 minutes longer. Increase heat to high. Add mussels; cover and cook 3 minutes. Stir in shrimp; cover and cook until mussels open and shrimp are opaque throughout, about 2 minutes longer. Discard any mussels that have not opened.

• Meanwhile, in large saucepot, cook pasta as label directs. Drain. In warm serving bowl, toss pasta with seafood mixture and parsley.

Each serving: About 410 calories, 25 g protein, 65 g carbohydrate, 5 g total fat (1 g saturated), 140 mg cholesterol, 588 mg sodium.

Test Kitchen Tip

To clean mussels, scrub well under cold running water. To debeard, grasp the hairlike beard with your thumb and forefinger and pull it away from the shell, or scrape it off with a knife. (Cultivated mussels usually do not have beards.)

Orzo with Shrimp and Feta

PREP 10 MINUTES   COOK 20 MINUTES   MAKES 4 MAIN-DISH SERVINGS

This sauce cooks up in minutes in your skillet. Watch the shrimp carefully and remove them as soon as they become opaque, so they don't overcook.

1½   cups (10 ounces) orzo (rice-shaped pasta)

1   tablespoon butter or margarine

1¼   pounds medium shrimp, shelled and deveined, with tail part of shell left on if you like

½   teaspoon salt

⅛   teaspoon coarsely ground black pepper

3   medium tomatoes, coarsely chopped

4   ounces garlic and herb-flavored feta cheese, crumbled (1 cup)

• In saucepot, cook orzo as label directs.

• Meanwhile, in nonstick 10-inch skillet, melt butter over medium-high heat. Add shrimp, salt, and pepper, and cook 3 to 5 minutes or until shrimp turn opaque throughout, stirring occasionally. Add tomatoes and cook 30 seconds, stirring. Remove skillet from heat.

• Drain orzo; toss with shrimp mixture and feta cheese.

Each serving: About 500 calories, 37 g protein, 60 g carbohydrate, 12 g total fat (5 g saturated), 197 mg cholesterol, 895 mg sodium.

Radiatore with Sweet-and-Spicy Picadillo Sauce

PREP 10 MINUTES   COOK 15 MINUTES   MAKES 6 MAIN-DISH SERVINGS

A zesty Spanish dish of ground beef, spices, raisins, and tomatoes, picadillo is traditionally served over rice. But, as this recipe shows, it's spectacularly good over pasta.

1   package (16 ounces) radiatore or corkscrew pasta

1   teaspoon olive oil

1   small onion, finely chopped

2   garlic cloves, crushed with garlic press

1/4   teaspoon ground cinnamon

1/8   to 1/4 teaspoon ground red pepper (cayenne)

3/4   pound ground beef

1/2   teaspoon salt

1   can (14 1/2 ounces) whole tomatoes in puree

1/2   cup dark seedless raisins

1/4   cup salad olives, drained, or chopped pimento-stuffed olives

    chopped fresh parsley leaves for garnish

• In large saucepot, cook pasta as label directs.

• Meanwhile, in nonstick 12-inch skillet heat olive oil over medium heat until hot. Add onion and cook 5 minutes or until tender, stirring frequently. Stir in garlic, cinnamon, and ground red pepper; cook 30 seconds. Increase heat to medium-high; add ground beef and salt and cook 5 minutes or until beef begins to brown, stirring frequently. Spoon off fat if necessary. Stir in tomatoes with their puree, raisins, and olives, breaking up tomatoes with side of spoon, and cook about 5 minutes longer or until sauce thickens slightly.

• When pasta has cooked to desired doneness, remove *1 cup pasta cooking water*. Drain pasta and return to saucepot. Add ground-beef mixture and reserved pasta cooking water; toss well. Garnish with chopped parsley to serve.

Each serving: About 470 calories, 20 g protein, 71 g carbohydrate, 11 g total fat (4 g saturated), 35 mg cholesterol, 775 mg sodium.

Lasagna Toss with Spinach and Ricotta

PREP 20 MINUTES   COOK 35 MINUTES   MAKES 4 MAIN-DISH SERVINGS

Here's real lasagna flavor in half the time. Simply boil the noodles while the sauce cooks, then toss with two cheeses and basil.

1   tablespoon olive oil

1   medium onion, finely chopped

2   garlic cloves, crushed with garlic press

1   can (28 ounces) plum tomatoes in juice

3/4   teaspoon salt

1/4   teaspoon coarsely ground black pepper

1   package (10 ounces) frozen chopped spinach

1/2   cup loosely packed fresh basil leaves, chopped

1   package (16 ounces) lasagna noodles

1/4   cup freshly grated Parmesan cheese plus additional for serving

1   cup part-skim ricotta cheese

• In nonstick 12-inch skillet, heat oil over medium heat until hot. Add onion and cook 10 minutes or until tender, stirring occasionally. Add garlic and cook 30 seconds, stirring.

• Stir in tomatoes with their juice, salt, and pepper breaking up tomatoes with side of spoon; heat to boiling over high heat. Reduce heat to medium and cook, uncovered, 8 minutes. Add frozen spinach and cook, covered, 10 minutes or until spinach is tender, stirring occasionally. Stir in the chopped basil.

• Meanwhile, in large saucepot cook lasagna noodles as label directs but increase cooking time to 12-14 minutes.

• Drain noodles; return to saucepot. Add tomato mixture and Parmesan cheese; toss well. Spoon into four pasta bowls; top with dollops of ricotta cheese. Serve with additional Parmesan, if you like.

Each serving: About 620 calories, 28 g protein, 100 g carbohydrate, 12 g total fat (5 g saturated), 23 mg cholesterol, 1,640 mg sodium.

Test Kitchen Tip

Stirring the fresh basil into the sauce toward the end of the cooking time ensures that it retains maximum flavor.

Pesto Ravioli and Peas

PREP 10 MINUTES   COOK ABOUT 6 MINUTES   MAKES 4 MAIN-DISH SERVINGS

With store-bought pesto and a no-cook tomato sauce, you can have dinner on the table in under 20 minutes!

1   pound refrigerated cheese ravioli

2   medium tomatoes, cut into 1/4-inch dice

1   cup loosely packed fresh basil leaves, chopped

1/8   teaspoon salt

1/8   teaspoon coarsely ground black pepper

1   package (10 ounces) frozen peas

1/4   cup basil pesto, store-bought or homemade

• In large saucepot, cook ravioli as label directs.

• Meanwhile, in small bowl, combine tomatoes, basil, salt, and pepper; set aside.

• Place frozen peas in colander, and drain ravioli over peas. In large serving bowl, toss the ravioli and peas with pesto; top with the tomato mixture.

Homemade Pesto

PREP 10 MINUTES
MAKES ABOUT 3/4 CUP SAUCE

2   cups firmly packed fresh basil leaves

1   garlic clove, crushed with garlic press

2   tablespoons pine nuts (pignoli) or walnuts

1/4   cup olive oil

1   teaspoon salt

1/4   teaspoon coarsely ground black pepper

1/2   cup freshly grated Parmesan cheese

• In blender or in food processor with knife blade attached, puree basil, garlic, pine nuts, oil, *1/4 cup reserved pasta water*, salt, and pepper until smooth. Add Parmesan and blend until combined.

Each serving Ravioli: About 510 calories, 23 g protein, 55 g carbohydrate, 24 g total fat (9 g saturated), 43 mg cholesterol, 705 mg sodium.

Each 3/16 cup Pesto: About 209 calories, 7 g protein, 3 g carbohydrate, 20 g total fat (5 g saturated), 10 mg cholesterol, 584 mg sodium.

Test Kitchen Tip

If you prefer, substitute refrigerated cheese tortellini for the ravioli.

Pasta Primavera

PREP 15 MINUTES   COOK 25 MINUTES   MAKES 6 MAIN-DISH SERVINGS

This dish is traditionally made in spring, when the first tender young vegetables appear—thus the name *primavera*, which means spring in Italian. We used fresh asparagus and sugar snaps and cooked them along with the pasta to save time.

1/2	cup heavy or whipping cream
3	tablespoons butter or margarine
4	ounces shiitake mushrooms, stems removed and caps thinly sliced
2	very small yellow squash or zucchini (4 ounces each), cut into 2" by 1/4" matchstick strips
4	green onions, thinly sliced
1	tablespoon chopped fresh parsley
1	package (16 ounces) fettuccine
1	pound asparagus, trimmed and cut on diagonal into 1 1/2-inch pieces
4	ounces sugar snap peas, strings removed
3/4	cup freshly grated Parmesan cheese
1/4	teaspoon salt

• In 1-quart saucepan, heat cream to boiling and boil 1 minute. Remove saucepan from heat and set aside.

• In nonstick 10-inch skillet, melt butter or margarine over medium heat. Add mushrooms and cook, stirring, 1 minute. Add squash and cook, stirring, until vegetables are tender, about 3 minutes. Remove from heat; stir in green onions and parsley. Keep warm.

• Meanwhile, in large saucepot, cook pasta as label directs. After pasta has cooked 7 minutes, add asparagus and sugar snap peas to pasta water. Cook until pasta and vegetables are tender, 3 to 5 minutes longer. Drain pasta and vegetables, reserving *1/2 cup pasta cooking water*.

• In warm serving bowl, toss pasta and vegetables with reserved pasta water, Parmesan, and salt. Stir in cream and mushroom mixture.

Each serving: About 491 calories, 18 g protein, 64 g carbohydrate, 18 g total fat (11 g saturated), 52 mg cholesterol, 462 mg sodium.

Pasta with Asparagus Pesto

PREP 20 MINUTES   COOK 15 MINUTES   MAKES 4 MAIN-DISH SERVINGS

Michael Chiarello, chef-owner of Tra Vigne restaurant in the Napa Valley and author of *The Tra Vigne Cookbook*, inspired this dish when he visited the *Good Housekeeping* test kitchen.

1 1/2   pounds asparagus, trimmed

1/4   cup olive oil

2   tablespoons pine nuts (pignoli), toasted

1/4   teaspoon ground black pepper

1   garlic clove, crushed with garlic press

3/4   cup packed fresh basil leaves

1   teaspoon salt

1/3   cup grated Pecorino Romano cheese, plus additional for serving

1   pound orecchiette or medium shell pasta

• If using thin asparagus, cut each stalk crosswise in half; if using medium asparagus, cut stalks into 1 1/2-inch pieces. In 12-inch skillet, heat *1 inch water* to boiling over high heat. Add asparagus and cook 5 minutes or until tender. Remove and reserve *1/2 cup of the asparagus cooking water*, drain the asparagus.

• Set aside 1 cup thin asparagus stalks or 1/2 cup medium asparagus tips. In blender at low speed, with center part of cover removed to allow steam to escape, blend remaining asparagus with oil, pine nuts, pepper, garlic, 1/2 cup basil, salt, and reserved asparagus cooking water until almost smooth. Add Romano cheese and blend until well mixed.

• Meanwhile, in large saucepot cook pasta as label directs.

• Slice remaining 1/4 cup basil leaves. Drain pasta and return to saucepot. Add asparagus sauce, sliced basil, and reserved asparagus, and toss until evenly mixed. Serve with additional Romano cheese, if you like.

Each serving: About 620 calories, 21 g protein, 88 g carbohydrate, 20 g total fat (4 g saturated), 7 mg cholesterol, 830 mg sodium.

Spaghetti Carbonara Pie

PREP 15 MINUTES   BAKE 35 TO 40 MINUTES   MAKES 6 MAIN-DISH SERVINGS

Try this for brunch or on a chilly evening—it takes just minutes to put together.

12   ounces spaghetti

4   ounces bacon (about 6 slices), cut into 1/4-inch pieces

1   container (15 ounces) part-skim ricotta cheese

1/2   cup grated Pecorino Romano cheese

2   large eggs plus 1 large egg yolk

1/2   teaspoon coarsely ground black pepper

1/2   teaspoon salt

pinch nutmeg

2   cups milk

• Preheat oven to 375°F. In large saucepot, prepare spaghetti as label directs.

• Meanwhile, in nonstick 10-inch skillet, cook the bacon over medium heat until browned, about 12 minutes. With slotted spoon, transfer bacon to paper towels to drain; set aside.

• In blender at low speed, blend ricotta, Romano, eggs, egg yolk, pepper, salt, nutmeg, and 1/2 cup milk until smooth.

• Drain pasta and return to saucepot. Add ricotta mixture, bacon, and remaining 1 1/2 cups milk, stirring to combine.

• Transfer pasta mixture to 2 1/2-quart baking dish (about 2 inches deep). Bake 35 to 40 minutes, until golden around edges and almost set but still slightly liquid in center. Let pie stand 10 minutes before serving (liquid will be absorbed during standing). Cut into wedges to serve.

Each serving: About 470 calories, 25 g protein, 50 g carbohydrate, 18 g total fat (9 g saturated), 154 mg cholesterol, 595 mg sodium.

Sunday Baked Ziti and Meatball Casserole

PREP 30 MINUTES   BAKE 25 MINUTES   MAKES 8 MAIN-DISH SERVINGS

A crowd pleaser that's easy to prepare. If you're in a time crunch, use four cups of your favorite jarred tomato sauce.

1   package (16 ounces) ziti or penne pasta

4   cups Big-Batch Tomato Sauce (page 30)

1   large egg

1   container (15 ounces) part-skim ricotta cheese

2   tablespoons grated Parmesan cheese

1   tablespoon chopped fresh parsley

1/2   teaspoon salt

1/4   teaspoon coarsely ground black pepper

8   frozen Lean Meatballs (page 30), thawed (see Tip) and sliced

1   package (4 ounces) shredded part-skim mozzarella cheese (1 cup)

• In saucepot, prepare pasta as label directs; drain. Return pasta to saucepot.

• Meanwhile, in 3-quart saucepan, heat tomato sauce, covered, until hot over medium-low heat. (If tomato sauce is frozen, add *2 tablespoons water* to saucepan to prevent scorching.) Add 3 cups sauce to the pasta in the saucepot; toss well. Reserve remaining 1 cup sauce.

• In medium bowl, stir together egg, ricotta cheese, Parmesan cheese, parsley, salt, and pepper.

• Preheat oven to 400°F. Into 3 1/2- to 4-quart shallow casserole or 13" by 9" glass baking dish, spoon half the pasta mixture; top with all the sliced meatballs. Drop ricotta-cheese mixture by spoonfuls evenly over meatball layer. Spoon remaining pasta mixture over ricotta-cheese layer, then spoon remaining 1 cup sauce over pasta. Sprinkle with shredded mozzarella cheese.

• Bake, uncovered, 25 minutes or until very hot and cheese browns slightly.

Each serving: About 470 calories, 29 g protein, 55 g carbohydrate, 13 g total fat (5 g saturated), 79 mg cholesterol, 1,040 mg sodium.

Test Kitchen Tip

Thaw frozen meatballs in refrigerator overnight. Or, place frozen meatballs on a microwave-safe plate. Microwave on Medium (50 percent power) for 2 to 4 minutes, until just thawed.

Big-Batch Tomato Sauce

PREP 15 MINUTES   COOK 1 HOUR
MAKES ABOUT 10 CUPS

Perfect for baked ziti and lasagna, this recipe makes 10 cups of mildly seasoned sauce. Heat 2 1/2 cups of sauce for each pound of pasta.

3   tablespoons olive oil

3   carrots, peeled and finely chopped

1   large onion (12 ounces), chopped

2   garlic cloves, finely chopped

3   cans (28 ounces each) plum tomatoes in puree

1   bay leaf

3/4   teaspoon salt

1/4   teaspoon coarsely ground black pepper

• In nonreactive 5-quart Dutch oven, heat oil over medium heat. Add carrots and onion and cook, stirring occasionally, until vegetables are very tender, about 20 minutes. Add garlic; cook, stirring, 2 minutes.

• Add tomatoes with their puree, bay leaf, salt, and pepper to Dutch oven; heat to boiling over high heat, breaking up tomatoes with side of spoon. Reduce heat; cover and simmer 15 minutes. Remove cover and simmer until sauce has thickened slightly, about 20 minutes longer. Discard bay leaf.

Each 1/2 cup: About 58 calories, 2 g protein, 10 g carbohydrate, 2 g total fat (0 g saturated), 0 mg cholesterol, 280 mg sodium.

Lean Meatballs

PREP 25 MINUTES   BAKE 15 MINUTES
MAKES 24 MEATBALLS

3   slices firm white bread, diced

1/3   cup water

1   pound lean ground beef

1   pound lean ground turkey

2   large egg whites

1/3   cup grated Pecorino Romano or Parmesan cheese

3   tablespoons grated onion

2   tablespoons minced fresh parsley

1   teaspoon salt

1/4   teaspoon coarsely ground black pepper

1   garlic clove, minced

• Preheat oven to 425°F. Line a 15 1/2" by 10 1/2" jelly-roll pan with foil; spray with nonstick cooking spray.

• In large bowl, combine diced bread and water. With hand, mix until bread is evenly moistened. Add ground beef, ground turkey, egg whites, cheese, onion, parsley, salt, pepper, and garlic. With hand, mix until ingredients are well combined.

• Shape meat mixture into twenty-four 2-inch meatballs. Place meatballs in jelly-roll pan and bake 15 to 20 minutes, until cooked through and lightly browned.

Each meatball: About 70 calories, 9 g protein, 2 g carbohydrate, 3 g total fat (1 g saturated), 24 mg cholesterol, 140 mg sodium.

Metric Equivalents

The recipes that appear in this cookbook use the standard United States method for measuring liquid and dry or solid ingredients (teaspoons, tablespoons, and cups). The information on this chart is provided to help cooks outside the U.S. successfully use these recipes. All equivalents are approximate.

METRIC EQUIVALENTS FOR DIFFERENT TYPES OF INGREDIENTS

A standard cup measure of a dry or solid ingredient will vary in weight depending on the type of ingredient. A standard cup of liquid is the same volume for any type of liquid. Use the following chart when converting standard cup measures to grams (weight) or milliliters (volume).

Standard Cup	Fine Powder (e.g. flour)	Grain (e.g. rice)	Granular (e.g. sugar)	Liquid Solids (e.g. butter)	Liquid (e.g. milk)
1	140 g	150 g	190 g	200 g	240 ml
$3/4$	105 g	113 g	143 g	150 g	180 ml
$2/3$	93 g	100 g	125 g	133 g	160 ml
$1/2$	70 g	75 g	95 g	100 g	120 ml
$1/3$	47 g	50 g	63 g	67 g	80 ml
$1/4$	35 g	38 g	48 g	50 g	60 ml
$1/8$	18 g	19 g	24 g	25 g	30 ml

USEFUL EQUIVALENTS FOR LIQUID INGREDIENTS BY VOLUME

$1/4$ tsp =				1 ml
$1/2$ tsp =				2 ml
1 tsp =				5 ml
3 tsp =	1 tbls =		$1/2$ fl oz =	15 ml
	2 tbls =	$1/8$ cup =	1 fl oz =	30 ml
	4 tbls =	$1/4$ cup =	2 fl oz =	60 ml
	$5 1/3$ tbls =	$1/3$ cup =	3 fl oz =	80 ml
	8 tbls =	$1/2$ cup =	4 fl oz =	120 ml
	$10 2/3$ tbls =	$2/3$ cup =	5 fl oz =	160 ml
	12 tbls =	$3/4$ cup =	6 fl oz =	180 ml
	16 tbls =	1 cup =	8 fl oz =	240 ml
	1 pt =	2 cups =	16 fl oz =	480 ml
	1 qt =	4 cups =	32 fl oz =	960 ml
			33 fl oz =	1000 ml = 1l

USEFUL EQUIVALENTS FOR DRY INGREDIENTS BY WEIGHT
(To convert ounces to grams, multiply the number of ounces by 30.)

1 oz	=	$1/16$ lb	=	30 g
4 oz	=	$1/4$ lb	=	120 g
8 oz	=	$1/2$ lb	=	240 g
12 oz	=	$3/4$ lb	=	360 g
16 oz	=	1 lb	=	480 g

USEFUL EQUIVALENTS FOR LENGTH
(To convert inches to centimeters, multiply the number of inches by 2.5.)

1 in	=		2.5 cm
6 in	=	$1/2$ ft =	15 cm
12 in	=	1 ft =	30 cm
36 in	=	3 ft = 1 yd =	90 cm
40 in	=		100 cm = 1 m

USEFUL EQUIVALENTS FOR COOKING/OVEN TEMPERATURES

	Fahrenheit	Celsius	Gas Mark
Freeze Water	32° F	0° C	
Room Temperature	68° F	20° C	
Boil Water	212° F	100° C	
Bake	325° F	160° C	3
	350° F	180° C	4
	375° F	190° C	5
	400° F	200° C	6
	425° F	220° C	7
	450° F	230° C	8
Broil			Grill

Index